SECRETS

of a

CELEBRITY

Piano

TUNER

JEFF BAKER

Contents

Introduction

When Shakespeare had to leave London for Stratford-upon-Avon due to the bubonic plague, he reportedly took advantage of the extra time he had to write Hamlet. In a similar way, though not necessarily to pen the greatest play ever written in the English language—though that would have been nice—on March 15th of 2020, when my piano tuning activities in the world of concert halls, theaters, and recording studios suddenly came to a grinding halt due to the COVID-19 pandemic, I decided to use my period of exile from New York City and went to Armonk-in-Westchester to gather together the many stories about my career that I had jotted down over the past forty years.

The first two weeks of March had been ridiculously busy. Broadway had just experienced its best year ever. Many new shows were about to open including the musical *Caroline, or Change,* winner of an Olivier Award in London, and *Girl From the North Country,* the much-anticipated new musical set to songs by Bob Dylan, both of which I had tuned pianos for during their rehearsals and previews, as well as Tina Fey's *Mean Girls,* where I'd been working at least once a week for the past year, that though had been doing quite well, had decided it was just too expensive to keep supporting a production in a dark theatre for what was rapidly looking like an indefinite period of time.

I'd survived the 90s when electric pianos began to replace acoustic ones, and later in the decade when synthesizers and home computers ended the need for large commercial recording studios. As well as the 2000s when soaring rents closed one piano shop after another, culminating in the recession of 2009, when sales of pianos took a dive from which they've never really recovered. But there were always enough pianos out there somewhere to service as well as those, like classical and jazz musicians, who would only perform and record on real ones, to keep me going.

This time was different. Especially as the original three-month closure became six and the possibility of the entertainment industry in Manhattan not reopening at all in 2021 reared its ugly head. Up until then, I had the privilege of being one of *those* guys who used the stage door or was whisked past the crowds and was immediately escorted by security or some official-looking person inside. To no longer be part of the crew preparing for the opening night of a Broadway show like *Hello Dolly* with Bette Midler or seeing the billboards and ubiquitous features in print and broadcast media announcing Taylor Swifts' new album knowing that I was scheduled to tune the piano that day at Sirius XM for its live debut with the superstar herself.

But more than simply feeling needed or in demand, I'd miss the excitement; the almost daredevil nature of what I would face on any given day. I'd go through the checklist in my mind: What condition would the piano be in? Have I brought everything I may need? Would I have the time, given the chaos I was certain to find, to do my job. Would the producer, the director, the artist, the stage-hands, or the staff at the venue be smart and professional or crazy and disorganized? It could happen and did. What about the traffic, the parking, the train, the subway…? One never knew what to expect.

I also knew that my job not only depended upon my skill as a piano technician but perhaps more importantly my ability "To keep your head when all about you are losing theirs," as Kipling wrote. Celebrities can be nuts. Their entourages, equally so. But for shows to go on, there must be a good number of competent people who can see what is happening, understand what was expected of them, and can quietly go about doing their jobs—people who know their place. I am proud to say that I have been and am one of these people.

I also happened to be, as you will soon discover, a person who takes note of things. It's easy to do when your office includes famous people like Meryl Streep, Tony Bennett, Frank Sinatra, Lady Gaga, and the many more who are included in this book. I have taken note of *a lot*.

I invite you to take this journey with me, visiting (or revisiting, in my case) some of the more notable moments of my long career as a celebrity piano tuner.

Most of all, let's have some fun, for as the Bard also once wrote: "What's to come is still unsure. Present mirth hath present laughter."

Sinead O'Conner

Incomparable

I rish singer and songwriter Sinead O'Conner, who achieved fame with her hit "Nothing Compares 2 You," wanted to record an album in the 1990s of songs that she grew up with and that inspired her to become a singer. The result was her third album titled "Am I Not Your Girl?" a collection of twelve jazz classics arranged for big band.

Phil Ramone, past producer of Frank Sinatra, Tony Bennett, Barbra Streisand, Billy Joel, and countless others—as well as a client of mine for many years (he's since passed)—was also brought onboard for the project. Since most of the notable albums from that genre were performed live (with the band and the singer recording at the same time), they decided to keep with tradition.

I was hired to tune and then stand by in case there was a problem with the piano—my area of expertise. But things didn't go as planned (which had nothing to do with me, thank God!) and Sinead went back to Ireland the next day without informing anyone. Since the studio time was booked and the band present and ready to record, they decided to go ahead, figuring that if Sinead wanted to add her vocals later, she would have that option. Eventually, she did join the collaboration, and after many hours and a whole lot of drama, the album was finally finished. A week or two later, Sinead appeared on SNL where she ripped up a picture of the Pope on live TV. Not even the great Phil Ramone knew what to do with that one.

Herbie Hancock

I Surrender

Herbie Hancock plays a very fine, handmade, Italian piano called a Fazioli. Being a customer and a famous artist, Herbie endorses Fazioli and in return, they provide him with an instrument and a tuner whenever he performs. Because there aren't many Faziolis around, especially their nine-foot concert grands, touting a two-hundred-and-fifty-thousand-dollar price tag, they must be sent from the closest dealership. And so it happened that I found myself in Boston for a "night of the stars" gala where I was scheduled to tune Herbie's piano at 11:00 a.m., but because the movers were late in arriving from New York City, I got bumped and kept getting bumped the entire day (even after the piano had arrived) due to sound checks, technical problems, unpunctual artists, and the general chaos that always accompanied rehearsals at events such as these. Except for Herbie, who was the featured performer, it was an odd lineup of people. Cable newsman Chris Matthews was there to interview General Petraeus, who had just resigned from the military due to an affair. (Matthews respectfully stuck to the subject of world affairs during the interview.)

There were ballet dancers, assorted musicians, various actors (you may or may not have heard of), who were all corralled into a small backstage area with a few ad hoc dressing rooms. Oh, and there was nakedness about (dancers don't care) and enough pot smoke to fill the air (nor do musicians). How strange to notice wisps of the pungent aroma encircling the former CIA director and commanding general.

Just before dinner break, someone announced, "Tuner!" It was finally my turn. But fifteen minutes later, that same person came over and said, "Stop. We need to start letting the audience in."

Argh.

I told Herbie what was happening, and he negotiated another fifteen minutes for me. The performance went well, but the moments leading up to it were stressful at best. Trying to prepare a piano in a half-hour for a major artist at a notable occasion in an important venue—and with the reputation of a prestigious manufacturer at stake, was cutting it too close. Never again, I said to myself.

So, a few weeks later, when I had a 10:00 a.m. appointment at another gala fundraiser for New York City's famous Roundabout Theater and they asked, "Can you wait an hour or so to tune?"

I answered, "Sorry, I have other appointments," and kept on working while every few minutes a guy wearing a headset would come over and ask, "How much longer does it take?" Then, just when it seemed like I was going to be able to complete my task, a couple of dozen tap dancers began their run-through, and I had to admit defeat. *Ok, you got me.*

"Will there be a break for lunch?" I asked. I learned there would be, and I arranged my return time accordingly.

Frank Sinatra

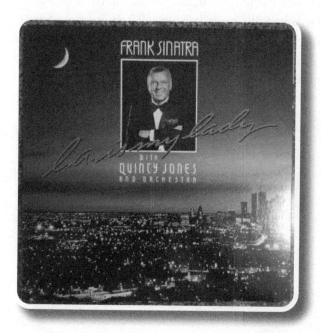

Ol' Blue Eyes

I have an album credit, sort of, within the liner notes of Frank Sinatra's *L.A. is My Lady.*

It read: "Sinatra's recording tonight. The band rehearses in the afternoon, 3 to 6, without the singer. Then, from 6 to 7, the studio falls becalmed, unglamorous. The only sound is that of a piano tuner going dwang-dwang-dwang through each of 88 keys."

Yes, that unglamorous "dwanger" was me! This was Sinatra's last studio album recorded live, quoted in its *New York Times* review as "the old-fashioned way, with a singer and skilled musicians recording together, all at the same time." (The two *Duets* albums that followed [his last] were extensively overdubbed.) Because of this, I was on standby in case there was a "piano problem" (there wasn't, thank God), and so I watched and listened to what Wikipedia coined "the most influential and popular musical artist of the 20th century." Together with the best musicians in the big band universe, they made musical magic. Still, it was hard to tell how inspired Sinatra was since he didn't stay very long. After all, this was his fifty-seventh album and though his signature phrasing was still there (and his light-up-the-room smile intact), he showed little interest in doing more than one take of anything or even listening to the playbacks, opting instead to be sent the mixes for his review.

Would he listen? Soon? Someday? Would he want to redo something? Add something else?

No one knew.

Miles Davis

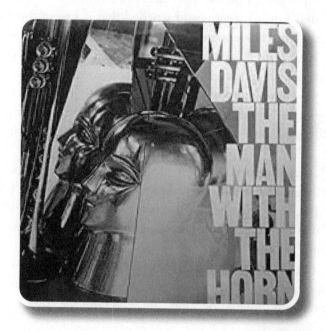

Miles and Me

After selling millions of albums for Columbia Records in the 1950s, 60s, and early 70s, and though still under contract, Miles Davis left music for five years (1975-1980) and lived in seclusion at his home in New York City. Then in 1981, with his contract up for review, he agreed to record again. But on the first day of his session, just twenty-five blocks south at CBS Studios, he didn't show. His excuse? His home piano was too out of tune for him to compose his music. So, I was sent to 312 West 77th Street to see what I could do. Though I could hear a TV blasting away inside, I couldn't get anyone to come to the door. It took a few phone calls to the studio for an emaciated Davis to appear wearing only an old bathrobe. He unlocked the door but immediately went back to watching his projection TV (only the red lens was working). Then, while looking around for the instrument in the detritus of what was once an elegant townhouse, I noticed that there were bullet holes in the walls, and though I didn't see a gun, I worried that if I went too far afield, he might forget I was there, think I was an intruder, and shoot me. Best to keep him within sight, I thought to myself. So, I cautiously approached him and asked to be shown to the piano.

Miles got up and took me over to something that had once been an upright but was now eviscerated, its innards strewn about.

"I'll need some parts from the shop," I said and got out of there ASAP.

Having taken years to get to the point where the label's superstar (cash cow) had finally agreed to come down and toot a few notes, and despite knowing his situation very well, the, quote, unquote suits at the label were upset with me. (Whatever. Not every cause is worth dying for.)

Later, I heard that they jammed something together with the personnel already available and Miles did eventually come in for some overdubs on what became *The Man with the Horn*.

Taylor Swift

Eye of the Storm

Taylor Swift gave two separate fifteen-minute performances at Sirius XM studios in Manhattan on the release dates of the albums *Reputation* and a couple of years later, *Lover*. My drill for both occasions was the same: Go into the glass-enclosed studio where the event was to take place, tune the piano, then take a seat outside until they were done rehearsing. Someone would inform me that my work had been approved, and then I could leave. Large black privacy curtains—later removed so the small "By invitation only" audience could see and hear (through speakers)—were also installed. On the first occasion, however, there was a small space between the panels of fabric that allowed me to discretely observe the goings-on, which interested me. It wasn't so much about monitoring my work or the desire to log another superstar sighting (I've seen enough) but out of a genuine curiosity to ascertain how Taylor was handling the worldwide mega-storm spinning all around her, especially when she seemed to be all that everyone, everywhere (particularly in the media), were talking about that day.

Well, based on the few moments I was able to observe of this exotic creature in her natural habitat, she seemed to be managing quite well. She rehearsed with her musicians calmly, competently, and most importantly, cheerfully. Most human beings couldn't handle fortune and especially fame of that magnitude. That was probably why most in her position became demanding, haughty, irascible and, not to mention, drug and/or alcohol dependent. There was also an idea floating around that a successful artist's best work was always done before they inevitably became corrupted by the lures of the world. But if an artist could stay centered, inspired, and remain fun to be around, while doing the one thing they seemed born to do, then I say God bless you, Taylor Swift.

The Kennedy Center

That's The Job

I n the same way that working in the pit at the Indy 500 is every mechanic's dream, tuning for a solo performance of a famous classical pianist in a major concert hall is an ultimate aspiration of mine. Dreams have a way of glorifying such things while overlooking the horror, though. If you leave the wing nut off the air cleaner on an old lady's Chevy, it might rattle around a bit. But if you do something similar on a racecar that goes two hundred miles an hour, the entire vehicle might fly off the track and not only kill the driver but several spectators as well. In other words, when working at the highest level of anything, you're expected to anticipate *everything*, which is impossible to do. But that's the job.

I was sent to The Kennedy Center in Washington, D.C. to tune a Fazioli concert grand piano that was being shipped from New York for a solo performance by that company's most esteemed classical artist. It was winter. The truck got caught in a snowstorm, and not only did the piano arrive late, but it was ice cold.

In an instrument such as this, there's a huge piece of cast iron inside that stabilizes the twenty tons of tension created by the strings, allowing it to be tuned and remain so for the time being. But because metal expands and contracts subject to temperature and though I fought like hell against this, when the piano was rolled out onto the stage and got hit by the heat of the lights, things immediately went south. And though I went out at intermission and did my best to correct the problem, the same thing happened again. After the performance, the artist immediately called Paolo Fazioli in Italy, and I was prohibited from ever working for that person again. (This was the only time in my piano-tuning career that I'd ever been fired. Let me state that in my defense.)

The New York Fazioli franchisee who had sent me, also got an earful, even receiving an email from the artist stating that when she had the "local" tuner (i.e., not some "big shot" from New York) in Chicago on the following night, everything went fine. That was also when I was told that there had been an unfavorable review of my work in the *Washington Post*, something concert pianists dealt with on a regular basis and maybe even got used to, though I doubted they ever did. It read: "The artist had her gleaming Fazioli shipped from New York without time to acclimate." It felt like a vindication for me, or so I thought (no one else agreed) but quite unfair to her. After all, she didn't arrange the move or create the weather!

But that's the job.

Billy Joel

Bon Appétit

I tuned pianos that were used in three of Billy Joel's albums: *Glass Houses* (1980), *The Nylon Curtain* (1982), and *An Innocent Man* (1983). In those days, it was not uncommon for a major artist to book a studio for six months or more to record an album. So, it was a great gig for me. Every morning before the Piano Man arrived, I'd tune his piano and any other keyboards necessary, such as a Fender Rhodes, a Yamaha CP-80, or a Clavinet that had been set out the night before. Then, later in the day, I'd call to find out if the instruments would be used that evening, and if they were, I would return during the dinner break and tune them again. Though we passed by one another often, Billy and I never spoke. We didn't have to. All our communication was done through his producer (the legendary Phil Ramone), an assistant, or some other person. Perfectly understandable. I wasn't there to call attention to myself and preferred being one less thing for Billy to worry about. During an evening towards the end of the third album (after years in his service) while waiting in the lounge for my touch-up to begin, someone came back with a message from the man himself: "Billy says 'tell the tuner not to eat the Chinese food.'"

Lady Gaga

Be Here Now, Now Get Out!

I was hired one night to tune a piano at 8:00 p.m. at Bemelmans, the famous bar in The Carlyle Hotel. After that, I was told to stand by until 10:00 p.m. to receive the artist's approval.

"Who's the artist?" I asked.

"We're not allowed to tell you," I was told.

Though a small venue, I arrived to find a large PA system, a drum set, various keyboards and guitars, trees of lights, a smoke machine, and an assortment of technicians and musicians packed into the diminutive area.

A man I recognized, who normally played piano at the bar, saw me. "You here for Gaga?" he asked, and the cat was out of the bag.

The event was called "The *New York Times* Celebrates the Greats," and Lady Gaga was slated to perform around 10:00 p.m. for ten or fifteen minutes. But since they didn't know what she was going to do, they prepared for everything. (The pianist was there in case she wanted to sing some jazz standards.) There were also people from the *New York Times*, hotel staff, and "Gaga" personnel all over the place asking everyone, "Who are you?"

When I said to one, "I'm the piano tuner," He replied with, "You can't be here, this area's reserved for VIPs."

Meanwhile, though I needed to start tuning, the drum tech was banging his kit, the audio engineer was ringing out his speakers, the guitar wrangler was doing his damnedest with a classic solo, and the smoke guy was fogging up the room. I probably should've said something about all the noise and whatnot, but I'd learned over the years it didn't do any good, especially at events such as this one. So, I just kept my head down and got to work.

By 11:00 p.m., cries of "She's here" filled the bar area along with "Everybody clear the room," which no one did (we just sort of hid) since it would be career suicide if your services were needed but you weren't immediately available.

Gaga entered the venue wearing a huge red dress. "Is this the piano?" she asked.

A chorus of "Yes, Gaga," shouted back at her. (Suddenly everyone was her point person!)

She sat down and started playing. "Fuck me," she said.

That was when I broke into a cold sweat. Thankfully, her problem was only that it took her a minute to remember the chords for her song, which she soon performed afterward.

With everything in order, I began slowly moving towards the door while continually asked, "Who are you?" and being told three or four more times, "You can't be here . . ."

Francis Ford Coppola

The Perfect Solution

An orchestra was assembled in midtown Manhattan to record the score for Francis Ford Coppola's movie *The Cotton Club*, which was being shot uptown at the same time. In normal situations, the music is added after a film is finished so that days or even weeks of very expensive recordings aren't made and never used. But as long as the checks cleared, no one at the recording studio was complaining. One morning, I arrived to begin tuning to find the inventory had increased by two more grand pianos. I was told to, "Tune one piano in-tune—one piano on the 'out-of-tune side' of in-tune—and one piano on the 'in-tune side' of out of tune."

I said, "Okay. No problem. But can I ask why?"

I was told it was "for authenticity's sake as pianos in the 1930s were poorly maintained."

A day or two later, I was instructed to tune only one piano correctly since the other two were driving everyone crazy and wouldn't be used, but to avoid confusion, I was to charge for three.

Made sense to me!

Chick Corea

Chick Corea
Akoustic Band

DIGITAL MASTER

A Grammy-winning Tuning

I spent a few pleasant days working for Chick Corea in New York City while he was recording the album *Akoustic Band*. He also had two other performances at the time: a Scientology convention and one at the Lincoln Center. A lot to do for one person in such a short period but for those few individuals in the world blessed with an extraordinary improvisational and pianistic talent (I'm reminded of Herbie Hancock, who I've also worked for), this was how they rolled.

Even though the work was demanding, Corea happened to be very pleasant, unpretentious, and professional. If he had an issue it was a reasonable one, and if you did your job well, he was appreciative. Chick even gave me a credit on the album that read: "Piano tuning and Regulation by Jeff Baker." Adding to the excitement, his album won the 1990 Grammy for Best Jazz Instrumental.

I'm not saying the two things were related, but I certainly didn't ruin his chances either!

Bo Derek

The Piano Man's Pianist

Aguy who helped me move pianos said he had a neighbor who wanted to meet me. "Why?" I asked.

"I told her about all the famous musicians you've worked for, like Billy Joel." he said. "As a tuner," I said to clarify.

Yet, he persisted. "She's an artist who studied at the Sorbonne. She also has a summer home in Rhode Island next to Taylor Swift's place and looks like Bo Derek," he said.

Looks like Bo Derek, huh? "Okay, okay, get her email, and if you're right, and she really does want to meet me for some reason, we'll get coffee or something."

Long story short, everything he told me about her was true, and when she walked into the room the whole place was abuzz with "Who's that?"

In my friend's report to *her* about *me*, however, he had left out that one crucial word: "tuner." Still, we seemed to get past that quickly and the conversation was easy, witty, and fun.

When I walked her to her car later, she very unexpectedly kissed me. A customary couple of days after this, I called to thank her.

"You're an interesting and charming guy," she said, "but I know what chemistry is, and we don't have it. And anyway, what I really went to find out was why Billy Joel needed a pianist."

So much for reflected glory.

Elvis Presley

Elvis's Scarf

My concert pianist friend, Maria Cisyk, had a Taiwanese student who was the personal assistant of a billionaire hotelier (not Trump, thank God), who'd been offered an opportunity to invest in Planet Hollywood franchises throughout the Far East. We all met at Maria's place in Carnegie Hall Studios, where we decided that the four of us would go undercover and check out the Planet Hollywood on 57th Street, it being right around the corner (since closed). The hotelier needed research if he was going to invest. Though it wasn't busy when we got there, the service was awful anyway. And the food, when it finally arrived, was cold. (I especially remember the rubberized fries.) The plates, silverware, and glasses were dirty, yet the bill was an astounding two hundred and fifty dollars.

"Why would anyone eat here?" the hotelier wondered aloud.

"They have Elvis's scarf," I said with excitement in my voice as I pretended that having the King's garment displayed in a glass case made whatever experience (good or bad) worthwhile.

But my humor seemed to escape him. "Elvis's scarf! Elvis's scarf!" he said loudly and repeatedly.

In that instant, he decided that since I apparently had no idea what a good restaurant was, he'd take all of us around the corner to Le Bernardin on West 51st Street.

As soon as we entered the famous French restaurant (with no reservations), the maître d' made a big fuss over the hotelier, preparing a large table and dispatching a small army of waiters who, for the next hour, would rush in and out of the kitchen with dish after dish of some sprig embellished with a swirly line of something or other—not to mention, a collection of wines, waters, and whatnots. How much did it cost? I guessed in the thousands.

A car was waiting after our meal to take the hotelier somewhere, so we said our goodbyes and off he went. Though we had been to two restaurants that afternoon—one with food that was uneatable and the other with food that was invisible, the three of us were still hungry.

Fortunately, there was a ninety-nine-cent-a-slice pizza shop on our way back to Maria's place, which for a dollar or two, gave us exactly what our empty stomachs needed.

Hal Prince

Goodnight Sweet Prince

Hal Prince, the legendary Broadway director and producer, died suddenly and unexpectedly in Iceland on July 31, 2019, while on his way back home to New York City. Just the day before, on July 30th, I had tuned the Steinway at his townhouse on East 73rd Street (my first time there). I was surrounded by the memorabilia of his life including twenty-one Tony's as well as various other awards, posters of his hit shows, scores, rave reviews of his work, and other emblems of his singularly extraordinary contribution to the theater. As I stood there, I wondered how it was that some people had such great success. *Why them?* Though I was often just steps away from where these same kinds of extraordinary things were happening, and while many whose opinion I respected have said I was truly talented, I hadn't had my breakthrough. Then something I saw on TV came to mind: Jerry Seinfeld had asked Seth Rogan why he never became a stand-up comic.

"I wanted to," he said to Jerry, "but then I met some people who *really* wanted to."

Hmmm.

That was my story, too, I realized. All the experiences I've had, not only through my craft but creative endeavors interested me, especially for the challenges they presented and the excitement and even notoriety they brought, but not to the degree that I was willing to make them my raison d'etre, like a Hal Prince had done in the theater.

Anyway, when at 3 a.m., only hours after I had been at Hal Prince's townhouse for my first and only time, I was rudely awakened by an iPhone notification from the New York Times saying that the great showman had passed, I lay there, trying to make sense of such a cosmic coincidence, but finding no rational explanation, simply said a prayer of gratitude for having been even a momentary witness to this amazingly important and inspiring life.

Holocaust Museum

A New World

The Holocaust Museum is a large, impressive building in Battery Park that provides views of the Statue of Liberty (the Mother of Exiles) and Ellis Island, where twelve million Jews and other immigrants were processed for entry into the United States from 1892 to 1924. There is also a railroad car out front that had once been used to transport what the Germans had called "Untermensch" (inferior people) to Auschwitz.

A large auditorium with a concert grand is contained within, which is where I come into the picture, and though a beautiful room, housing a wonderful piano, the experience of traveling down there is always sobering, as it should be.

My job completed, I was back on the subway after one of my visits, where a group of schoolgirls (four to be exact) wearing light-blue blouses and gray pleated skirts were visiting with each other. One of the girls appeared to be Asian, the other Latina, the last two African American, and Caucasian. They were giggling about God only knew what, the way teenage girls often did the world over, when in the company of their friends.

A Muslim man seated near me wearing a long white tunic and an embroidered turban was reading from his prayer book. An Orthodox Jewish woman wearing all black, with wig and scarf, entered pushing a baby carriage, and the Muslim man got up and offered her his seat.

What was so extraordinary to me was just how ordinary a scene this was, but at the same time, how hopeful. I was struck by how ignorant, wanton, and unnecessary that historical train (the one bound for the death camp) was and would forever be. The people on the subway coexisted just fine simply by being considerate.

What I saw on that day made me realize that "A New World" was always just an act of amity away.

John Lennon

Dear John

If you were in New York City between 1971 and 1980 while John
Lennon was living there, you were always hoping to run into him.
The closest I came to this goal was when I was sitting in the lounge of
a recording studio where he was working, waiting for another session
to end so that I could do my job. I was there listening to a group of
musicians who were on a break from their session with him. A guitarist was complaining that the Beatle member had taken a pick out
of his case without asking.

"Did he say anything?" one band member inquired.

"Yeah," the aggrieved person replied, "He said, 'Relax, you're working.'" Everybody laughed, yet the annoyed man sat there with his brow furrowed.

I was struck by how quickly "familiarity breeds contempt" as they say. When given the opportunity to be around those we dream of getting to know, we soon start having problems with them.

I hung out as long as I could, but John never emerged by the time I got the call to do my thing.

By the way, picks seem to be an obsession with guitarists. I once owned a small music store in Queens, where I sold two picks for twenty-five cents. I was told by a customer that they were sold for three for twenty-five cents in Manhattan.

"Then go there," I said. "Buy two subway tokens and waste half a day to save five cents." Later, a friend of his told me that's exactly what he did!

Meryl Streep

WITH MERYL STREEP AS ALICE
DIRECTED BY JOSEPH PAPP
CHOREOGRAPHY BY GRACIELA DANIELE
THE PUBLIC THEATER

God-given

I was working at The Public Theater recently, where a poster from a 1979 production of the play *Alice in Concert* was on display. It was something I saw in rehearsal while waiting to tune a harpsichord there.

I was so completely mesmerized by the lead actress's performance, especially the psychedelic scenes which gave me flashbacks, that I asked someone, "Who's that girl?"

They replied, "Her name is Meryl Streep."

Since it was before she was a world-famous actress, this meant little to me, but I remembered thinking that there were some people who could do certain things so miraculously well, especially in the arts, that their success seemed preordained.

Michael Jackson

Great, Even in Absentia

S tars can afford to be late, but superstars don't have to show up at all. I once waited for hours for Michael Jackson at a studio for a recording session with him, until someone finally called to inform us that Michael was sorry, but he wouldn't be in that day. He had to buy some old leather-bound books for the library in his new house.

Frank Sinatra was also very elusive, especially later in life (maybe he had had enough), but unlike the King of Pop, he made no excuse at all—even a lame one.

During the making of his first *Duets* album (1993), when it was discovered that Frank would be in New York City between his performances in Atlantic City and Connecticut, a studio was booked, an orchestra was hired, and every accommodation was made (even a private dressing room with a carton of Camels, a Zippo lighter, and a bottle of "Jack" was supplied). But an hour or so after the session was scheduled to begin, with everyone in their places and ready to go, Frank's chauffeur called to say that he had just gone to the airport and put Sinatra on his plane bound for Palm Springs.

"What should we do?" someone frantically asked Phil Ramone (the producer). His reply, "Record! I'll tell him he was great!"

Yoko Ono vs. James Taylor

The Latest

U sually, the star was the last to arrive for their session, which made sense. They had more important things to do then watch guys like me banging around. Still, there were times when they showed up early and even came into the studio while I was tuning.

Yoko Ono did just that.

"Isn't anybody here yet?" she'd asked.

And though technically I was "somebody," but not somebody important in a world-wide sense, I took no offense.

"No, I don't believe so," I'd said.

Soon someone from the studio came in and rescued her. "Oh, Yoko, we're so honored to have you here. Is there anything we can get you?"

And Yoko went on her way.

If I was not at the piano but standing off to the side of a venue and someone famous would come over and introduce themselves, not knowing who I was or what my duties were, I'd do my best to help them out.

"I'm the piano tuner," I'd say to clarify things. This revelation freed them up to say something like, "Isn't anybody here yet?"

Once this happened with James Taylor, who said, "Hello, I'm James." "Hi. I'm the piano tuner," I said, expecting the usual response.

But instead of the customary reaction, James seemed to sense the whole dynamic and said, "We need you!"

An Assisted Living Center

Beauty is in the Ear of the Beholder

A classical pianist was to give a recital at an assisted living center and asked me if I could go by and check the piano—and if necessary, tune. The piano was in predictably awful shape and had many mechanical issues as well. They must've had musical programs there frequently for as soon as I began striking the keys, residents started drifting in like zombies and gathering around the piano. Normally nothing like that would bother me, but these people were expecting to be entertained. Not my job.

I went looking for a staff member. "I'm working on the piano, but I think the residents think I'm here giving a concert," I said.

"That's what they do," a female staffer said with a dismissive flip of her hand.

So much for that, I thought. While I worked my way through the keys, some of the residents sat motionless, some swayed, and some even sang along, as much as, since I wasn't playing anything recognizable, such a thing was even possible.

One woman huffed. "You stink at the piano," she said in a rather loud voice that she kept using to shout her disapproval.

"I'm not playing, I'm fixing!" I said.

Soon she left, thank God, along with most of the other residents as well. But one man stayed for the entire event, and when I began packing up he came over and said, "Thank you. That was so, so beautiful."

A Teen on A Train

Ahhh, Youth

I was sitting on a train returning home from my piano-tuning jobs in the city, when an attractive young girl, maybe in her late teens or early twenties, wearing a sliced-up pair of daisy dukes, plopped down in the seat across from me, even though there were plenty of other empty seats available. Our knees touched (hers being bare from the torn-up jeans). She immediately launched into a blow-by-blow description of all the scandalous things she'd been up to in the city.

I said nothing, just kept my head in my phone while making an occasional nod of polite recognition, the way one does when listening to the ramblings of a crazed teenager. Not only did she keep talking, but I noticed her flirting as well—always a boost for a man's ego. Then, I wondered if she was some kind of call girl working the northeast corridor.

Suddenly she caught herself. "I'm sorry. I'm doing all the talking. Did you ever do anything fun when you were young?"

Like a tire with a puncture, my ego deflated.

An Art Gallery

Art for Art's Sake

I received a call to tune a piano at an art gallery, but when I arrived, the piano had been incorporated into part of an art installation. How would I service it without going down as the philistine who destroyed a great masterpiece? But lo and behold, the artist had considered this problem and had made a piano-shaped frame to which they attached brightly colored fabric, made rigid with varnish in such a way that the entire assembly could easily be lifted off the piano and later replaced. It was a miracle and the first time, to my knowledge, that an accommodation to practicality had ever been made in the history of art—modern art, anyway.

On Broadway

Good to Know

Travesties, a play by Tom Stoppard, that included an onstage piano that would be used as a functioning prop (meaning it needed to play) was about to open on Broadway.

"Please come and tune during our lunch break," the man who hired me said.

I arrived at noon. What I found was a one-hundred-and-fifty-year-old piano that was in disastrous shape. Sometime later, I still had various glued pieces of the instrument spread out all over the stage ten minutes before the rehearsal was set to resume.

"What are you doing?" asked the stage director. "We only need the area around middle C."

Turned out the piano wasn't meant to work. Not really. The actor was directed to play a little tune, hitting the high and low sections before saying, "I really need to have this fixed."

If only someone had directed *me*.

Christie Brinkley

Star Power

When the digital revolution hit and everyone could afford to have a recording studio in their home, the big facilities in town went out of business. Within a year, I went from having a dozen accounts to a mere five. Suddenly, I was forced to look for other means of gainful employment. Around that time, I also got a call from Billy Joel's office.

"Can you come out to Billy's new studio at his home on Long Island and tune his piano?" the man asked.

"Sure," I said, "but I'll have to charge my day rate since that's how long it will take me to drive out there, do the job, and return home."

"We'll get back to you," he said.

Thankfully, they did get back to me, but surprisingly, they made no mention of my terms, only adding, "Billy and Christie will both be there." He was referring to Christie Brinkley, Billy's supermodel wife at the time.

I didn't know what kind of value one could place on that sort of thing, especially since I'd seen Billy dozens of times over the years. Even though possibly meeting a ten-time *Sport's Illustrated* swimsuit issue cover model would certainly have been more memorable, it wasn't something I'd go that far out of my way for.

"I'll still have to charge my day rate," I said. I never heard from them again.

A Five-Star Hotel

Right Away, Ma'am.

S ome of the fancy hotels in New York City have grand pianos in their suites that are regularly tuned. They also have apartments. A nice way to live if you can afford it!

One day, while I was working in one of those suites, and though it was midday, the apartment dweller next door started banging on her wall, complaining about the noise. She must've also called the front desk for within minutes, someone came and told me to cease and desist until a staff member had taken the woman down to the dining room for a snack.

After completing my job there and while waiting for the elevator, the "complainant" and a female staff member strode past me.

"Why do I have to walk under that thing?" the woman said.

"You mean the scaffolding, ma'am?" the female staffer asked. "We're so sorry, but they're repairing the ceiling."

The woman replied with, "Well, it's an eyesore. This used to be a good hotel." "I'll speak to management immediately," the staffer said.

I knew she wouldn't, and I suspected she knew she wouldn't, either.

Apartments at that hotel began at ten million dollars with a twenty-five thousand per month maintenance fee, which came with an expectation that all those well-healed enough to afford to reside there be free from all annoyances, especially and without exception, the truth.

Mount St. Vincent College

BMOC (Big Man on Campus).

I was working at the College of Mount Saint Vincent in the Bronx where a sign-up sheet was posted asking students to submit names for the "Most Popular Male Student" award aka "Mr. Mount."

I trust you see the irony.

Philippa Soo

Thank You, Next?

To be fresh, the piano is normally tuned as close as possible to a performance, which usually takes place after the final rehearsal. This has awarded me many wonderful experiences while waiting to begin my work. One such event was a private recital during which Tony Bennett conducted a sound check. Another was when I spent a half hour seated near composer Stephen Sondheim at City Center while Jake Gyllenhaal ran through his *Sunday in the Park with George* performance, where I was a witness to Jake's anxiety and Sondheim's reassurances. The actor had nothing to worry about. And that wasn't just my opinion. According to the *New York Times:* "Gyllenhaal was a searing theatrical presence who had the vocal chops to deliver one of Mr. Sondheim's richest and most intricately composed scores with the rapt determination of someone trying to capture the elusive."

Hearing that rehearsal had provided me with one of those moments when all the anxieties of life were suddenly silenced by the power of the arts. I lived for them. But sadly, they were also too rare, and so were the people who were able to convey them.

There were two audition rooms equipped with pianos that were tuned every two weeks in the Actors' Equity building near Times Square, where I'd watched hundreds of hopefuls line up for a chance to show the world what they had to offer. Aspiring singers, dancers, and actors alike would wait for hours to go and stand before those who would determine their professional fate. More times than not, they would hear, "Thank you, next," before they had even begun.

On rare occasions, though, someone would enter the audition room and not come back out right away, which would set the entire cue waiting outside abuzz.

"Are they that good?" someone would ask.

"Did they just get the part I was hoping for?" someone else would say.

Of course, there was also the random, "How come I never even get to finish my song?"

When Phillipa Soo (who is now a Broadway star), the original Eliza Hamilton in the musical *Hamilton*, went to her first audition, not only was she asked to continue, but the producer there was rumored to have said, "Everyone will want her. The only question is, who will get her first?"

About a year ago, while waiting for a rehearsal for a children's music and art charity benefit to end and while listening to one very talented artist go through one number after another, Soo got up and sang "Children and Art," which was also from Sondheim's *Sunday in the Park* musical.

Some of the lyrics were:

You would have liked him Mama, you would
Mama, he makes things

Mama, they're good
Just as you said from the start Children and art
Children and art

I wept.

After Philippa had left the stage, and as if something sacred had taken place, the room remained quiet, until the poor actor who had to follow her, went up on stage and began. The man did well but was unable to silence all the murmurs about the *It Factor* exhibited by the one who had preceded him. Everyone knew what the *It Factor* was when they saw it—and the mystery of why some had it and others didn't was always in question: If you kept putting yourself out there, was it possible to acquire?

A famous pianist and teacher once said, "In the end, there is a final test that only one in a thousand will pass for it involves something that can never be taught—the 'profundity of soul.'"

The Juilliard School

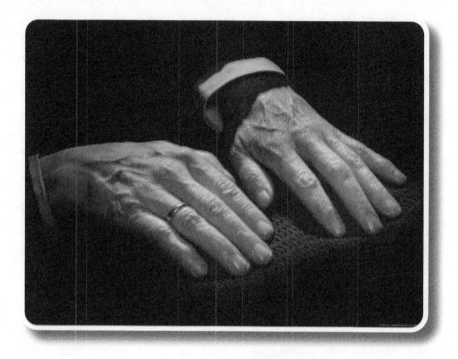

Rachmaninoff's Hands

I was tuning a piano for a new client (a concert pianist) who had gotten my name from somewhere or another. While there, the man noted that I had large hands (an octave and a third). The thing I'd learned about hands was that some very famous pianists such as Rachmaninoff had grand ones (reportedly, an octave and a half), making their compositions even more challenging than they already were. I shared a story with my client that was told to me by my dearly departed pianist friend, Maria.

She said, "After getting into Juilliard on a scholarship and being assigned to the most coveted piano professor there, I was understandably excited."

At her first lesson, however, the legendary professor said, "I'll teach you because you are musical, but you'll never have a career. Your hands are too small."

Determined to prove him wrong, Maria prepared some really "stretchy" Rachmaninoff for her next session and played it well, but when she looked up, her teacher was asleep.

Then, when he awoke, he asked her to go look for his prize pupil, who, rather than coming for his lessons, had taken to frequenting pool halls. (Welcome to the big time!)

Turns out, my new customer was Maria's classmate, and not only did he know her *and* her professor, Mieczyslaw Munz, but the identity of the prodigious but wayward student as well.

Ladies and gentlemen, I give you the now world-famous and eight-time Grammy-winning, Emanuel Ax.

A Realtor

Every Excuse

I received a frantic call from a realtor who had an imminent closing on a property for an estate whose two beneficiaries (the decease's son and daughter) hadn't done anything about the contents, including a large grand piano.

"I can deal with everything else," she said, "but I need you to remove and store the piano ASAP."

Not long after that, the son called me, very upset with the realtor. "How can she do this? She knows I have ADHD," he said. "What about your sister?" I asked.

"She's passive-aggressive. Even if she's there, she won't help."

I found his diagnosis spot on. On the day of removal, when no one answered the door, the realtor used her key to let us all in, and there was his sister, sitting at the kitchen table, complaining to someone over the phone that since her good-for-nothing brother wasn't helping her, it was his fault, not hers, if they lost the sale!

Sirius XM

Today's Featured Artist...

I was tuning a piano at SiriusXM Studios in Manhattan, when a woman came in and wanted to try the instrument. I logically assumed that she was the performer scheduled for that day, so I asked her to be brief for I still had work to do.

The woman started pounding out some truly mad Scriabin.

"I will need the highest treble section sharper, the bass notes slightly lower, and a twenty-one-and-a-half-inch-high stool," she said.

When was I supposed to do all that? I thought to myself.

The producer for that day's session arrived soon after. "Who are you?" he asked the woman.

"I may be playing here in a week or two," she said to him.

Meanwhile, someone announced that Chris Isaak, the artist whose group it turned out we were preparing the piano for, was on his way up from the lobby.

The woman told the producer she needed a few more minutes and refused to leave. In fact, security had to take the woman out and keep her muzzled until Chris Isaak, none the wiser, had passed by and she could be escorted out of the building.

Tony Bennett

Revenge is Sweet

When I first met Tony Bennett, he was just as nice as the guy I had seen on TV. If he noticed me tuning the piano before a recording session or a performance, he would say, "Thanks, the piano sounds great."

If his pianist was present and within earshot, he or she would nod in agreement, especially Ralph Sharon, his longtime accompanist.

Still, I wondered whether Sharon really felt that way or was obligated to agree with his boss.

There was another pianist who sometimes worked with Bennett, especially as Sharon got older (Ralph retired in 2002 at the age of ninety-one), who didn't seem to agree with Tony at all and instead of a nod, would reply with a scowl.

Maybe he was just grumpy, I thought to myself.

One day, I received a call from Phil Ramone's office to go ASAP to Club 53 at the New York Hilton Hotel. Phil was helping Peggy Lee (age seventy-two), who, though wheelchair-bound, was still determined to perform as the *New York Times* put it "despite her precarious health."

"Please. The piano's in rough shape," the person said over the phone.

When I arrived, Phil announced, "Thank God you're here."

I noticed right away that the same peevish pianist from my time with Tony Bennett was also Lee's accompanist for the evening. Not only did he not say anything, but the man looked at me as if he had suddenly smelled something awful. Still, I didn't know if his problem was with me personally or, like some very difficult pianists, with tuners in general.

Some weeks later, that same petulant pianist saw me on the first day of another recording session that he was working, and I got word from the studio that he would be using his own tuner the next day. This happened from time to time (after all, some people had chefs they preferred or doctors and so on). His snub did feel pointedly critical, however.

The next morning, I received a call from the studio. The pianist's preferred tuner hadn't shown up. I was asked if I could hang out somewhere nearby in case there was a problem with the piano. Since I was in the neighborhood, and because they offered to pay me, it just so happened that I could.

A little while later, they called again and said, "The pianist came in, assumed his own tuner had been there, went over to the piano where he played a few chords, and said, 'Now that's the way a piano should sound!'" It was still tuned from *my* work the day before, of course, but we all agreed it would be best if that remained our little secret—and it had, until now.

A Recital Hall

Who Goes There?

I was subbing for a colleague on a recently restored Steinway at a recital hall in upstate New York, where the community was known for taking in and caring for individuals with special needs. When I arrived, the door was open, so I let myself in.

Suddenly, a man appeared out of the shadows. He blurted out something that I didn't quite understand, and then he disappeared. He must've had a speech impediment, I reasoned.

A half-dozen other people soon showed up, presumably to arrange things for the upcoming event. One person came over, took my tools off the table next to me, and put them on the floor. Another stood on the piano cover I had placed on the apron of the stage. Someone else started singing along with the notes I was striking ... or tried, anyway.

Finally, a young woman came over and said, "I hope we aren't making too much noise," and this being a reasonable sentiment, made me wonder if she might be in charge. That was until another girl got angry with the woman for bothering me, causing her to sob uncontrollably.

"Stop blubbering and hurry up. We're leaving." someone else said.

And just like that they were gone, except for the first man I had encountered who continued lurking about and hiding each time I looked his way.

Later, I asked my colleague, who often worked there, if he knew the man. "Yes," he said, "that's the security guard."

A Trade Show

Compose

" to create, write or arrange "

Not Gonna Be So Easy

I've been composing music for most of my life, beginning with rock and roll in the 60s, folk music in the 70s, and theatrical and classical music more recently and had many subsequent successes with it.

I'd learned that if you stepped out of your comfort zone and did anything creative, like paint, write, or compose, someone may be kind enough to say to you, "The world really needs to hear (or read, or see) this."

When I was starting out, one such kind soul assured me that if I made some cassette tapes of my music, there would be a big demand for it. Inspired to be a success, I went a step further and rented a booth at a music trade show. For most of the show, no one seemed very interested in my work. They'd just walked by without giving me a passing glance. The tepid responses continued until one fellow hurried over to me. My heart raced. The man seemed very interested in my work until he asked point-blank, "Can you record over this?"

So much for instant fame and a sure-fired fortune.

Concert Tuning

A Flea's Sneeze

Tuning pianos for performances and recordings, as I've been doing for more than forty years, can be exciting, but depending on the artist, it can also be a little *too* exciting, bordering on exhaustion. This could happen when a perfectionist would profess, "Can't you hear that? It's like a buzzy kind of zingy sound," and try as you might, you can't.

Recently I heard a great quote attributed to Franz Mohr, the legendary tuner for Horowitz and many, many others. He described a particularly difficult concert pianist this way: "She could hear a flea sneeze under the snow!"

Dmitriy Cogan

Coming In Loud and Clear

Sondra Lee, a great friend, legendary actress, dancer, and drama-turge, as well as a collaborator of mine on things theatrical, had a CD (a signed copy) of a violinist and pianist on her coffee table.

The name of the pianist was Dmitriy Cogan, which caught my eye.

It wasn't because he was well known but because my dearly departed friend and concert pianist, Maria Cisyk, used to speak amus-ingly of a child prodigy with the same name. According to Maria, the child was so absentminded that after his lesson, he'd always turn off the lights on his way out, leaving her sitting alone in the dark.

I looked closer at the CD, specifically at the performer's bio in the liner notes. One line stuck out to me: "San Francisco Conservatory... studies with Maria Cisyk." I thought of my friend and smiled. It seemed our souls had reconnected in the most unexpected *and* amusing of ways!

Fifth Avenue

Yes, Your Majesty

I was working on a piano on the second floor of a six-story mansion on Fifth Avenue, when I heard the lady of the house downstairs. Her voice echoed down the vast marble entryway.

"What's that noise?" she asked.

Someone, who I assumed was the house manager said, "We're having the piano tuned." "Was it on the schedule?" the woman asked.

"Yes," the manager said.

"Well, why didn't I see it?" said the regal woman.

Silence followed or if they spoke, I couldn't hear them.

A few minutes later, a housekeeper sat on the stairs near where I was working. I imagined her assignment was to watch that I don't steal anything. I got the feeling that this sort of court intrigue went on in "royal households" such as this one all day long, for the maid sat there with a look on her face that said, "I've just got to remember, I'm getting paid for this."

Frank Wildhorn

Never Give Up?

In 1989, I wrote a musical titled *Psyche,* which was based on the Greek myth of the world's most beautiful girl (named Psyche) and who Venus (the goddess of beauty), being jealous, sent her son Cupid to curse. Things didn't go as planned, and Cupid fell in love with her, instead. It was funny and poignant, and the music was impressive, in my own humble opinion.

I sent it around to all the usual places and received the typical rejections. That all changed when Musical Theater Works, a well-known developer, called me back saying they were interested enough to give me a staged reading for two nights at the Douglas Fairbank Theater on 42nd Street. Afterward, though not giving me any reason, they said they wouldn't be continuing with the project. (Oh, except for the director who had a great idea ... not! He'd said, "Why don't you make it about Marilyn Monroe?" Like that was something that wouldn't take another year to do!)

One day, I was tuning the piano at a well-known theater composer's apartment and thinking about my musical. As I worked, I wondered if maybe there was something I hadn't thought of that would have helped me along with my show's success.

I took a break and Googled "Getting your musical produced," and the top article was titled: "Give up!"

Ready for the cosmic kicker? Frank Wildhorn, the man for whom I was working at that moment, was featured in the article as an example of a "teachable moment." It was in the second paragraph, which read: "Despite having established himself on Broadway, none of Wildhorn's shows ever turned a profit."

Google/YouTube

That Way Madness Lies!

I went to the YouTube and Google New York City headquarters, a labyrinthine assemblage of new but mostly empty offices that occupied six floors above Chelsea Market. I was there to tune the piano in a recording studio stocked with a rock and roll musician's wish list of vintage guitars, amps, and too many other instruments to name, all provided as a perc for the exclusive use of their employees.

"They just have to put it in their calendars," said the man who (thankfully) had been sent to show me the way.

After countless staircases, elevators, and endless passageways, we arrived at our destination only to find that another fellow was already in there.

"I have the room," said the man in question. "No, I have it," said my guide.

Both men then opened their Google calendars and discovered that the app had not been set up to warn users of duplicates.

"Seems to me someone around here should be able to fix that," I said considering where we were.

"Yes, that would be me," said the current occupant (apparently, he was on the calendar team). Calendar-man left with my helper tagging along (presumably to debug the thing).

A few minutes later, I remembered that just a day or two prior to this, my own Google calendar had erased all my old appointments, which I had needed to create my invoices. I hoped to run into one of those two men on my way out to tell them that but never did.

In fact, I didn't encounter anyone except one bleary-eyed programmer who was wandering around supporting his laptop with one arm while typing with the other hand. God only knew how many hours and days he'd been at it. I suddenly wondered how I was going to escape this maze I was in and asked him, "How do I get out of here?"

The programmer just stared at me as if his ability to communicate with other human beings had long ago left him.

I did eventually make it out, but the experience of the crazy world of technology we now find ourselves inextricably caught up in, was noteworthy.

The Greene Space

The operations manager at Greene Space (WQXR, New York Public Radio, NPR, etc.) and I had developed a little private banter over the years since I'd been tuning there. "You know we use those notes," he'd say, referring to the ones I was working on.

Then, on my way out, I'd fain anger with him and shout, "See what you can do with *that*," implying that I may have sabotaged something.

One day while I was leaving, I said my portion of the usual sarcastic banter but didn't notice that the producer for that evening's event, which were the Avery Fisher Awards (a big deal, which goes on PBS's NYC/ARTS, etc.) was within earshot.

Considering we were in mixed company, the operations manager just stared at me as if to say, "Have you lost your mind?"

The producer raised his eyebrows, probably wondering what my problem was and what his might soon be.

That was my Greene Space faux pas.

The Joyce Theater

Message From the Beyond

Soon after arriving at The Joyce Theater, a premiere dance performance venue in Chelsea, for my final appointment at the end of a long and ridiculously frustrating day, that evening's choreographer came over, interrupting me, and said, "My brother, our jazz pianist, is late but asked me to tell you to do a complete tuning, not just a touch-up." Of course, she had no way of knowing that that was the last straw, but it was.

"I've prepared thousands of pianos over the last forty years for people like Herbie Hancock, Chick Corea, and every other jazz pianist you've ever heard of, so I think I know what to do!!"

The woman withered away, in a "What's that freakin' guy's problem?" sort of way.

A few minutes later, the choreographer's brother arrived, but rather than showing any interest in my work, he immediately, excitedly, and vociferously started riffing about all the different pianos in town he liked and didn't like and why.

"Great, now I've got to try and do this while this jive cat chews my ear!" I grumbled to myself.

Then, out of the blue, he said that his all-time favorite piano was a Steinway that was on loan to the Fat Cat Club while their Yamaha was getting rebuilt. It just so happened that it was *my* loaner and *my* rebuilding job. The Fat Cat Club was also where my pianist friend Maria's daughter Samantha had married a jazz guitarist. Then, I discovered that this guy was at the said wedding. In fact, they were all old friends, including with his sister.

When the universe wanted to teach you something, like "Always be humble," I learned that day, ya gotta be cool, man.

Leonard Bernstein

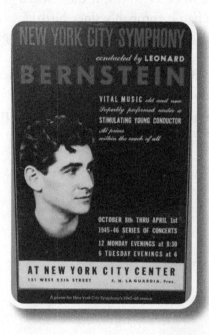

Words of Comfort

I was working in the Green Room at City Center, where this poster of a young Leonard Bernstein from 1945 (he would have been twenty-seven at the time) caught my eye. I thought back to 1979 when I had traveled with my meditation teacher, Sri Chinmoy (I was part of the choir group), to Lenny's apartment at The Dakota on 72nd Street to sing an arrangement of "Eternity's Singing Bird," which was written by Sri Chinmoy for Lenny. It was a beautiful piece for a soulful occasion. But if you've ever had any hopes for a career in the arts, like I did back then, a face-to-face encounter with true genius, especially of the world-class variety, could be quite disheartening.

Bernstein had perfect pitch, a photographic memory, and the ability to look at an orchestral score and instantly play a reduced version at the piano. In other words, if there was a gift that was innate to a musician, he had it (probably since birth).

After we left, I asked the guru why God gave some people everything.

"Maybe Mr. Bernstein was a cantor in a former life, very sincere but extremely unlucky," Sri Chinmoy said.

Whether it was true or not, picturing the maestro's previous misfortunes made me feel much, much better.

South Street Seaport

Rules are Rules, Even Ones Made Up on The Spot.

I arrived an hour early for a 1:00 p.m. appointment at the South Street Seaport (for a Sheryl Crow concert), and not seeing any reason to wait, I started tuning. It was a good thing, too, because at 1:00 p.m., a guy from the union came over and informed me that no one was allowed on stage during their lunch break which had started at that moment. I mentioned that though I was done, I had, in fact, been scheduled for 1:00 p.m. The man said it didn't matter, rules were rules. Most entertainment venues in New York City were governed by these rules even though they're quite arbitrary.

There was a foreman at the Lincoln Center, who didn't like hearing the piano being tuned while he worked, so he decreed that it must be done *during* his meal break and only after he'd a chance to get some distance away.

SNL

Watch Your Step

When I worked for Carrol Musical Instrument Rental Service (1979-1982), we'd occasionally deliver equipment to the set of Saturday Night Live that I'd have to tune, such as an upright piano for Bill Murray's lounge-singer sketch and the like. I didn't know much about the show or even that it was such a sensation (just another stop as far as I was concerned) until one Saturday night, when a group of friends invited me over for a watch party. The night's entertainment was, lo and behold, Saturday Night Live.

"Wait. I had to step over that guy the other day," I said (referring to John Belushi whom I had discovered conked out in a room, near where I needed to work.)

My friends stared at me with wide eyes and jaws agape. They thought that was amazing, but I didn't think very much of it at all.

What they didn't realize was that early every morning, when I went out to follow up, tune, and repair the deliveries for the day,

I'd often have to maneuver over and around dozens of people, some famous, who'd been up all night for a rehearsal or recording. Something, that having been a Hippie, I was quite accustomed to, as everyone in those days would just party until they were unconscious and then "crash" right where they were (a popular and more accurate name for going to sleep—since no one in those days "went" anywhere, like a bedroom, for instance, to do so). Many also, despite what was going on all around them, might lie there until noon or even dinner time, especially members of rock bands who rarely saw the light of day, or if they did, were too stoned to recognize that that was what it was.

I once had to step over, around, and through the entire lineup of Aerosmith along with many friends and lovers who, after ostensibly having worked all night on their new album, had simply crashed.

Nowadays, due to steaming, no one, no matter how successful, would dare book a studio for weeks if not months at a time and get little or nothing done. For while the most popular artists and groups of the 60s, 70s, and even 80s, could earn up to $3/album sold, Snoop Dog, for example, recently confessed to having made only $45,000 for one billion (!) streams.

The Cathedral of St. John the Divine

How Soon They Never Forget

The Cathedral Church of St. John the Divine on the upper west side of Manhattan is the largest Gothic cathedral in the world. Along with being a working church, it is host to many new-age and oftentimes paganistic happenings such as Paul Winter's Annual Winter Solstice Celebration. It's an ideal space for these types of events since it can contain multitudes of people, and its extreme reverberance makes everything sound trippy. This latter fact is also why it's a very challenging place to tune a piano since every struck note bounces around the walls for what sounds like an eternity.

Once, while I was tuning for such an event, a priest came out and asked if I could take a short break as they had a memorial service that would soon end in one of the small chapels that branched off from the main sanctuary. I understood why. If someone even moved a chair across the marble floor there it could be deafening, so I agreed to pause.

About ten minutes later, the same priest came back and said, "The Bishop says you can begin."

"What about the Pope?" I asked, thinking this would tickle his funny bone. Not the case. My remark had struck a nerve, instead.

"We're Anglicans," the priest said with a somber expression.

In 1535, because the Pope wouldn't annul Henry the VIII's marriage to Catherine of Aragon, Henry left the Catholic church and formed his own, declaring himself "The Supreme Head of The Church of England," aka The Anglican church.

As the priest stared down at me, I realized that only in the world of religion could a subject still be touchy after nearly five hundred years!

Steinway Hall

Get Down with RPP (Rich People Problems).

A woman frantically calls from the showroom at Steinway Hall. She needs to decide between a *limited-edition* Steinway grand piano with a price tag of $155,374.42 or a normal model for a mere $71,698.50, and she needs to decide right away. Today is the last day of their sale, you see.

What a life.

Stephen Sondheim

Sondheim Knows

Years ago, I was hired to give lessons in computer music publishing to a group of copyists at Chelsea Music, where the scores for most of the Broadway shows were prepared by hand. The whole assignment was a little sad since the student's penmanship was so beautiful. It was also sad because they could see the writing on the wall as changes made during a show's development—even something as simple as a key change to accommodate the vocal range of a particular performer—which they profited mightily from the time this took to redo everything by hand, would soon be done for a pittance with a keystroke. Understandably, my class wasn't very attentive.

Stephen Sondheim was one of their clients and would send in handwritten pages consisting of a melody with lyrics, a few chords, and a suggestion or two of a phrase for a particular instrument. I thought this was a kind of cop-out until I worked on a musical myself. I realized that since hundreds of things could be tried and tossed while putting together a show, doing anything more than the minimum of what was presently required, was a waste of time.

A Street Vendor

Beggars *Can* Be Choosers

Having back-to-back tuning appointments with no time for lunch, I decided to grab a bagel from a street vendor on my way to the subway. I got there just in time, too, as he was packing up for the day.

"Here, just take 'em," the vendor said handing me a half-dozen or so bagels in a paper bag.

"How much?" I asked.

He waved me off. "Save your money. I was gonna throw them out," he said.

"Thanks. I'll give them to the homeless," I said, as if he gave a hoot what I did with them or was impressed that I considered myself to be another Mother Teresa.

As soon as I got on the train, a tattered-looking man came down the aisle.

"Dime, nickel, penny, anything to eat or drink, even a little water?" he said.

"Here," I said, offering the bag.

"What is it?" he asked. "Bagels," I said.

"Are they spicy?" he asked.

"They're bagels!" I answered incredulously.

"Sometimes bagels are spicy," he said, handing the bag back and continuing on his way.

The Unions

Economics Local 101

I have a client, Bonndy Pianos, who provides tuning and other services to the many Broadway theaters that keep rehearsal pianos on their premises. While grateful for the work, I've often wondered—especially when I'd be hired to go to the same theater, like Tina Fey's *Mean Girls,* once or twice a week—why the shows don't just use a portable electronic keyboard that doesn't have to be tuned.

Well, I learned the reason.

Anything electric requires a union electrician (with a minimum of four hours @ $100/per hour) to plug and unplug it. Also, since an amplifier would be needed, a sound engineer must be retained at a similar rate. Not only that—the people in the show wouldn't be allowed to set the keyboard up and break it down themselves—meaning two more union members would be required. So, it was far less expensive to have two stagehands move an acoustic piano to its rehearsal position after the performance (as part of their normal shift, so no overtime) and back into the wings when they arrived at their usual hour the following day.

A piano should be tuned after it's moved, of course, which is where I come in.

So, I guess I should just shut up and take the money, especially if I ever want to work in this town again.

Valentine's Day

Isn't It Romantic?

M y day looked easy: I had two stops on 56th Street, one stop at 4th Street and Avenue A, and my last stop at 6th Street and Avenue B. The only problem was the clients kept changing the times for their appointments, which ultimately meant going back and forth over the span of fifty blocks. To add to my misery, it was pouring rain out. Still, I somehow managed to be punctual, even though no one seemed to care, especially at my last stop, a nightclub, where they were preparing for that evening's Valentine's Day show. It was a spoof of *The Sound of Music* in which the nuns were lesbians and Baron Von Trapp wanted to sodomize everyone, especially the prudish governess (played in the movie by Julie Andrews). I don't think she'd like this version—but who knows? Having been in the theatre since the age of thirteen, she'd probably seen it all.

The lights kept going off and on, taped music was being played, parody songs being sung, and since there was no dressing room, nudity was afoot as well. Still, I was used to this kind of cacophony and started tuning, even trying to convince myself that a higher purpose was being served.

"If I ever have to go to hell," I'd reason, "I'd be well prepared."

Oh, their skit had a happy ending. The Baron got his wish, which, in their telling, was cause for a great celebration.

A Veteran Golfer

Our Little Secret

An elderly man wearing a military cap with numerous pins and insignias attached, joined my golfing twosome one day, along with his son.

"I was a fighter pilot in WWII. I'm ninety-six years old. I have a new girlfriend. She's eighty-one," he said. "What do *you* do?" he asked.

"I'm in the piano business," I said.

"My new girlfriend has a piano," he said.

He was an interesting golfer who would get out of his cart, take a swipe at his ball, get back in, and have his son drive over to wherever the ball had landed. Then, he'd pick it up and speed ahead to where the rest of us were, and drop it there, where the process would repeat itself.

After seven holes or so, the decorated veteran had had enough, but something was on his mind that he needed to share before he left. He called me over. "If you ever go to my girlfriend's place, don't tell her what I told you. She thinks I'm eighty-three."

A Wanted Poster

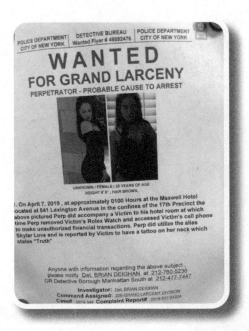

Calling All Cars!

The security services at some of the New York City hotels distributed notices with descriptions of various troublemakers who they wanted the staff to look out for. One such "Wanted" poster took the cake. It said that a girl named Skylar Love was picked up in a hotel bar at 1:00 a.m. and taken by a guest to his room where she removed his Rolex and hacked into his bank accounts using his cellphone. The poster also said the perp could be identified by the "Truth" tattoo on her neck.

Just goes to show, you can't judge a book by its cover.

Beethoven

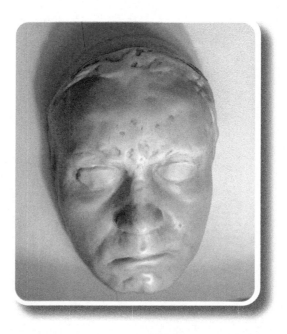

Face to Face with the Man

I did a little face time while tuning at a client's home with a casting of Beethoven's life mask of 1812, age forty-one (he died in 1827 at age fifty-six). He didn't look so happy that day. But I guess it was hard to smile while trying to breathe through a straw with your face covered in plaster.

World's Worst Customer

Curses!

I got a call from a homeowner many years ago who said, "How much does it cost for a piano tuning?"

"Thirty-five dollars," I said. (This was many, many years ago.)

When I arrived at the job, the owner didn't just want me to tune her piano, she also wanted me to dust inside the instrument, vacuum the area under and around it, and go over the scratches with some Old English oil which she provided, all the while she sat a few feet away from me shouting out questions like, "Why are you hitting the keys so hard?"

A day later, the woman called me back and said, "My brother is here, and he can't even push down the keys. I'm cancelling the check. I curse the day I met you!"

Every career has a few pits in the pie.

Duke Ellington

Respect!

I worked for Bonndy Pianos on Duke Ellington's personal piano at the National Jazz Museum in Harlem. It was an ordinary instrument with extraordinary vibes.

The Early Train

Calm Before the Storm

I had an early tuning appointment in the city, so I took the 5:40 a.m. train, which I normally didn't mind since there were always plenty of empty seats, and I enjoyed the peace and quiet. But at the very first stop, a type A businessman entered the train and plopped down next to me with a can of energy drink (which he didn't need), a bag of nuts, and a copy of the *New York Times*. He peeled the wrapper off his straw, tossed it aside, then jammed it into his can, and began sucking the life out of his beverage. He continued to suck even after the contents were long gone. Then the man discarded the empty container (which rolled around on the floor as the train swayed) and started chomping handfuls of nuts like a chipmunk stocking up for winter.

How his teeth didn't shatter was beyond me. After that, the man flung open his paper and proceeded to jab his elbow into my side with each turn of the page.

When we arrived at Grand Central, he jumped up, sprinted down the aisle, and disappeared into the city's abyss. Maybe I should have said something about the mess he'd left behind, but I was so glad he was out of my life that I simply offered a prayer for his family and his co-workers, and all those others who, unlike me, were unable to escape from this man's circle of madness that day and every other.

Geneva Camerata

My Dream Date

I wanted to see the Geneva Camerata, a classical ensemble with musicians who incorporated movement into their performance. The director of programming where they were playing was a good friend of mine and provided me with two complimentary tickets. I contacted several people I thought might be interested in going with me, but no one accepted.

I emailed the director. "My friends don't know what's good for them, or they do and it's not an evening with me. So, unless you know a supermodel with a thing for seventy-year-old men, my other ticket is available."

When I arrived at the event, the seat next to mine was vacant.

"So?" I said to the director, who was seated in my row a few seats over. "Where is she?" He answered me with nothing more than a wink.

Soon, a thirtyish and very attractive Michelle Dockery looking English woman (Downton Abbey accent and all) took the seat next to mine. I learned she was an agent and more interested in working the room than in anything I could offer, but I still had to give my friend kudos for his impish spirit!

Piano Moving

Do You Believe in Magic?

When you are making an estimate for a piano move (something I've done a lot of) it's important to know how difficult it will be, i.e., how many steps I would need to take into the house, how many steps inside, how many turns, etc., to know the number of men to send and how much time to allot. Realizing that being honest can result in a higher fee, customers tend to lie.

One such customer said, "We have just three steps in the back," but when we arrived, there was nothing behind the house and a whole series of steep and very awkward stairs in the front.

"We intend to have three steps put in back there someday," said the homeowner.

"And someday *we* intend to have a magic ray gun that we can point at a piano and levitate it," said one of my co-workers.

Touché.

Metro-north

I was driving past a reservoir amidst glorious foliage on a beautiful Sunday morning on my way to catch the train for a tuning job in the city. Sundays were normally my "day of rest," but I figured that at that hour and on that day, it'd be a quiet trip. I was also hoping it would give me time to focus on a book I was writing.

On the train, a couple behind me was awkwardly silent with each other. No small talk of any kind.

Then, the woman said, "I'm going to my sister's."

"I'll take you if you can stand being with me for more than an hour," said the man. I could feel the hostile vibes.

Across the aisle, a Bengali woman was shouting into her phone as though trying to bridge the gap between her and her phone companion in the subcontinent. A couple of rows ahead of me and on my side of the train, sat a man who appeared sloshed (probably from his Saturday-night revels). He was also on his phone and, with slurred speech, was trying to explain to his boss why he couldn't come in that day but shouldn't be fired for it.

All at once the drunken man spilled a take-out cup of hot coffee on himself and launched into a flood of obscenities as the beverage's brown stickiness started coming under the seat towards my feet.

The idea for a new book dawned: *The Human Condition and Other Lost Causes.*

Old Willy

Do Not Go Gentle...

In 1979, after my two-year apprenticeship at the Manhattan School of Music, I had a job tuning and repairing pianos and other keyboards for Carroll Music Instrument Rentals, whose clients included the halls, stages, and studios in Manhattan. The job was often very intense with only minutes between the time the trucks finally arrived (due to traffic, parking, and the dozens of stops they had to make every day) and when the events went live. But I was young and loved the excitement and, more importantly, I always managed, somehow, to finish my job on time.

Those were also the days before synthesizers and computers with VSTs (Virtual Studio Technology) which meant that there were dozens of recording studios everywhere, especially in and around Times Square, where an old guy named Willy tuned their pianos. Sadly, Willy had reached the point where any kind of noise would cause him to stop whatever he was doing, waddle over to the offending party (even the session's VIPs), and shout, "Let me know if I'm bothering you," right up in their face.

And so it was, since I was able to do my job quickly, competently, and much, much less dramatically (unlike Willy), that most of his work soon became mine. In fact, there was so much of it that I left Carroll's and went out on my own.

Willy believed I stole his clients and though I visited him a few times at his apartment to try and patch things up, he very likely took that idea to the grave.

Lately, due to my own advancing years, I've been wondering if I'll be any more accepting when it's my time to be put out to pasture. Although, in my own defense, I haven't yelled at a VIP...yet.

A Nursing Home

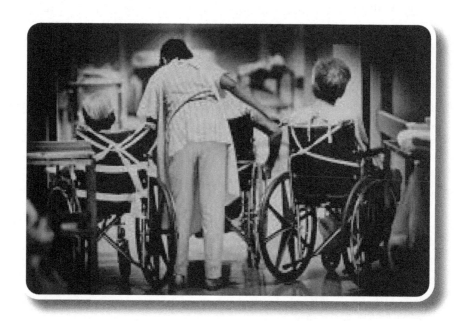

My Savior Cometh

I received a call to tune a piano at a New York City-run nursing home. There were two sets of doors with separate buzzers to get to the security desk and a metal gate that had to be unlocked by a guard to enter the ward. The halls were crowded with patients aimlessly wandering about, except for one very old guy with a walker who lurched by as fast as he could as if trying to escape or die, though sadly in his case, the liberation of death may have been the only option to be free he had.

The piano was in horrible shape. I did what I could while another man, who must've played it regularly, stood close by nervously wondering if I was trying to break the piano so he'd never be able to perform again. (Perhaps they sometimes did that kind of thing there.) Later, while waiting at the gate to be let out, an old woman grabbed me around the legs.

"You've got to get me out of here," she said, her eyes pleading.

Two burly orderlies in white smocks quickly appeared and pried her loose. I was free to go and more determined than ever to do everything in my power to never end up in a place like that.

The Commissioner Hereby Declares

OCCUPANCY BY MORE THAN
213 PERSONS
OR BY
227 PERSONS
AS REHEARSAL ROOM
OR BY
93 PERSONS
AS REHEARSAL ROOM
OR BY
90 PERSONS AS
DINING ROOM
IS DANGEROUS
AND UNLAWFUL

Certificate of Operation No. 220563959
COMMISSIONER, DEPARTMENT OF BUILDINGS
CITY OF NEW YORK

Count Me In

If you're the two hundred and fourteenth, the two hundred and twenty-eighth, the ninety-fourth, or especially the ninety-first person in the room, you better know exactly what it is you intend to do! Or to be safe, don't bring a sandwich.

Ol' Broadway

Ladies and Gentlemen, an Old Man

When a Broadway musical moves into the theater, a set of temporary and oftentimes very steep stairs, with no handrails as well, are constructed to bridge over the orchestra pit so that everyone can quickly get from the seats (that have been covered with tables and workstations) to the stage and back. There's also frequently a rehearsal piano up on stage that needs tuning, which is where I come in. Ascending the stairs is fine, but because of my bad knees, I look for a safer way down.

Noticing this, the stage manager at one such production said, "Don't worry, we'll help you," and in full view of the entire company, he sent two burly stagehands over to take my hands, one on each side, and help me down the stairs.

Oh Boy! In that moment, I had become ancient.

Parking

Ah, New York

I had an early Sunday morning job at a hotel on Madison Avenue. Confident I'd find parking on the street, I drove into the city. When I was near my destination, however, I ran into two movie shoots, a production for the Tony Awards, and the National Puerto Rican Day parade, not to mention a convoy of tow trucks already out scooping up cars at $175 a pop. But then I came upon a sign at a garage only a block away from where I needed to go that read: "PARK HERE FOR PARADE. REGULAR RATES APPLY."

That's decent of them, I thought.

When I entered the garage, the attendant said to me, "It's seventy-five dollars for the first hour."

"Is that your regular rate?" I asked.

The attendant said, "No. Our regular rate is thirty-five dollars. Seventy-five dollars is our regular *parade* rate."

Hmmm.

People and Places

Place Disgrace

I had a tuning appointment that took me to Ossining (location of the infamous Sing Sing prison), but the customer insisted she lived in neighboring Milltown. Many people in less affluent parts of Fairfield County would say they lived in Greenwich and in areas of Westchester County, and especially around White Plains, West Harrison was claimed. Even better, I met a woman so ashamed of living in Yonkers that she made up her own name of Dorchester. Adding to the ruse, she gave me out-of-my-way directions through posh Scarsdale to get there!

The Quiet Car

Shhhh...

The Metro-North Railroad provides a Quiet Car where conversations and especially phone calls are expected to be kept to a minimum. And if you don't mind a longer walk to and from the last car of the train (where this is usually located), it makes for a much more pleasant trip. Bear in mind, however, that having deliberately taken the time and trouble to select this option, your fellow passengers will become very upset, even vocally so, if you break the rules, especially if your phone rings, which was what happened to the man seated next to me.

"Sorry," he said, "I have to take this, it's my wife."

The man was trying to speak as softly as possible, but I was still able to deduce from his conversation that his wife had told him that he didn't have to go with her to her sister's place the previous weekend, even though he had asked her several times if she was sure—her answer always being yes, he was now in big trouble for not going.

Soon, we went into a tunnel and the man lost his signal, which he seemed certain would be interpreted by his wife to mean that he had hung up on her.

"Shit! Shit!! Shit!!!" he said in an increasingly louder voice.

"Shhhh!!!" replied all the passengers in unison.

The man should have told his wife that he was in the Quiet Car, I thought to myself, naively imagining that there was a rationale for this kind of problem.

Acknowledgements

S o, there it is—my story of some of the more memorable moments of my career, which hopefully you enjoyed and, God willing, more tales will come. As I reflect on all my years, certain experiences stick with me more than others, and my heart is filled with gratitude, especially for the miraculous way that whenever I stepped out of my comfort zone and tried to accomplish something special, uniquely qualified people would come into my life and help me.

When I was an apprentice in the piano maintenance department at the Manhattan School of Music, I formed many lifelong relationships with workers from the Steinway factory in Astoria, Queens, who shared their knowledge passed down from generations of craftsmen (dating back to 1853) who had worked there. When I was interested in musical composition, I was introduced to Maria Cisyk, a concert pianist who had taught at Juilliard, Yale, and the San Francisco Conservatory of Music, and who became my muse and champion. For theater, an organization called Mainstreet Musicals saw enough promise in one of my projects to send me to Sondra Lee, a famous dramaturge, member of the Playwrights and Directors division of The Actor's Studio, veteran of dozens of Broadway shows and famous movies, and a friend to luminaries such as Jerome Robbins. In spirituality, it was Sri Chinmoy, an Indian guru with the most ancient lineage and exalted level of consciousness I'd ever encountered. I'd first met Sri Chinmoy in 1972, when I was twenty and remained with him until his passing in 2007. (In a cosmic sense, he is still with me to this day.)

What was it aside from their wisdom and their real-world experience that distinguished all these amazingly accomplished teachers? It was never about the money for them. It was always about the work. Somehow, they all knew what it was that I was trying to learn, express, and accomplish, even before I did, and they selflessly guided me there.

Many have also tried to help me with my literary efforts, but I must make special mention of Tricia LaRochelle, my editor for this book SECRETS OF A CELEBRITY PIANO TUNER for she could also see the mountaintop through my clouds of mismatched tenses and dangling participles, and she put me back on the right path whenever I tried to chase an improper noun into the woods. (Though she still might have some work to do on my overuse of metaphors.)

I thank and continue to thank them all!

In this crazy world that we live in, it's the people and the connections that help us along. I've been blessed by those I've been privileged to know as well as others I meet every day. It's also very important to be ready and open to learning—an eternal student, as they say. When I met with Sondra Lee for the first time, she looked at my materials and said, "This is pretty good for someone who doesn't know anything," before she proceeded to tear my work apart. Another of her more notable assessments was, "All you've got here is you trying to make everyone see how smart you are. Tell the story! No one gives a shit about your neediness."

My final words: I hope you the reader, whoever you are, find your own path and with it, the people who can help you reach your goal(s). Even more important, I hope that you are able, by listening and learning, to make the most of whatever talents you have and opportunities the world sends your way.

Thank you for reading and hopefully laughing, something we could all use these days. Oh, and please tell everyone you meet how smart I am. Except if you run into Sondra Lee, who hates that kind of thing!

About the Author

A premier concert technician preparing pianos for performance and recording, Jeffrey Baker is also a contemporary classical composer who has penned more than one hundred pieces of music for piano, soloist, choir, chamber, and full orchestra. In 1988, the Manhattan Chamber Orchestra at Symphony Space performed his piano concerto *Rhapsody for a New Age*. In 1990, Musical Theatre Works at the Douglas Fairbanks Theatre performed his musical *Psyche*. In 1997, Jeff was honored with a "Meet the Composer" lecture and concert at Western Connecticut State University. *The Music of the Zodiac,* Jeff's classical journey through the zodiacal signs for chamber orchestra has received tens of thousands of downloads. Jeff wrote a piece for choir titled "The World Sings For Peace," which consisted of the word "Peace" in twenty-seven different languages, which was performed at the United Nations. A reading in 2018 at the Actors Guild in New York City of his play about Leo Tolstoy, adapted from Gorky's *Reminiscences* and co-written by Sondra Lee, featured Dick Cavett.

Made in the USA
Las Vegas, NV
24 October 2024